1982

THE RETURNS OF LOVE

*Letters
of a
Christian
Homosexual*

D1447248

ALEX DAVIDSON

*InterVarsity Press
Downers Grove
Illinois 60515*

© *1970 by Inter-Varsity Press, England*
Second American printing, December 1977
by InterVarsity Press, Downers
Grove, Illinois, with permission from Universities
and Colleges Christian Fellowship,
Leicester, England.

InterVarsity Press is the book publishing
division of Inter-Varsity Christian Fellowship,
a student movement active on campus
at hundreds of universities, colleges and schools of
nursing. For information about local and
regional activities, write
IVCF, 233 Langdon St., Madison, WI 53703.

Distributed in Canada through InterVarsity Press,
745 Mount Pleasant Rd., Toronto M4S 2N5.

ISBN 0-87784-698-7
Library of Congress Catalog Card Number: 70-131594

Printed in the United States of America

. . . I think there is no unreturn'd love, the pay
is certain one way or another,
(I loved a certain person ardently and my love
was not return'd,
Yet out of that I have written these songs.)

WALT WHITMAN

*To Peter
and others who have helped*

Foreword

This book, the chronicle of an intelligent, sensitive Christian man's struggle to overcome homosexual impulses, may prove enlightening and helpful to a large segment of the Christian community. It raises a number of pertinent questions.

First, does a vital, biblically-based faith provide immunity from mental illness? One cannot help but be impressed by the author's strong commitment to Christ and his concern for carrying out the moral imperatives of his faith. Yet he also describes vividly the deep-seated and overwhelming nature of his homosexual desires.

Second, if the Christian suffers severe emotional conflict, should he seek psychiatric help or draw exclusively on his spiritual resources? The book's discussion of this issue and the conclusion the author reaches will be helpful to many confronting this dilemma in their own lives and in the lives of family and friends.

Third, if a Christian seeks psychiatric help, is it necessary for him to find a psychiatrist who shares his spiritual convictions? The author's conclusion—that this qualification in a doctor, though helpful (in some cases it may actually impose a barrier), is not necessary and that the emphasis ought to be on a doctor's skill and competence—is both wise and medically sound.

Fourth, is homosexuality sickness or sin? Does Scripture express any view on the subject? The author's thinking here is both medically and scripturally valid. He views his homosexual *condition* as *illness,* and this conforms with the preponderance of current medical opinion. This opinion classifies homosexuality as a form of psychopathology that warrants medical intervention. The author, however, views homosexual *activity* as a direct *transgression* of God's law—which certainly conforms with the strong prohibition of homosexual behavior in the Old and New Testament documents. In no way does he resort to the easy rationalization of many today who deny the pathology of homosexuality, who refuse to consider its moral implications and who tend to view it as a form of sexual expression that merely "differs" from the statistical norm. Such attitudes, though appearing humane and altruistic, act to destroy the well-being of the homosexual. They not only discourage his seeking available help, but also encourage him to resign himself to a life that clinical evidence reveals to be increasingly lonely and frustrating—regardless of how permissive and accepting our society becomes.

Fifth, what attitudes should the church have toward the homosexual? The book alludes to the insensitive ear—not to mention the closed door—which the homosexual often encounters within the Christian community. Such rejection, as in cases I have observed, intensifies the anguish, the pervasive loneliness and utter despondency that haunt the homosexual, and not infrequently lead to suicide. Christ, while taking strong action against sickness and sin, reached out to both the sick and the sinner with understanding and compassion. The church can ill afford to do less.

The wide coverage afforded homosexuality in the news

media, resulting from the recent activity of national homosexual organizations and the participation of female homosexuals in the Women's Liberation Movement, makes this book particularly timely and significant. As homosexuality becomes more acceptable for discussion, the church will undoubtedly become more aware of the problem among its members. As a matter of fact, the church may find a surprisingly large number of people within its congregation struggling with homosexual impulses. This ought not to be surprising, for at least two reasons: (1) The loneliness, the intense need for human contact and the image of himself as a misfit cause the homosexual to see the Christian community as a refuge and a possible source of acceptance and comfort. (2) Recent research findings disclose a statistically significantly higher incidence of cold, rejecting fathers within the family background of homosexuals, producing within many a yearning for a warm, accepting, loving father. The appeal of Christianity in meeting this particular emotional need is obvious.

The book expresses an optimistic, hopeful note that cure will be forthcoming. Is this optimism justified in light of modern clinical psychiatry? Can one reasonably hope for complete cure? As with all psychotherapy, success depends on multiple factors, the motivation of the patient being an important one. Most homosexuals tend not to be motivated. Unlike neurotics, they obtain a certain release of tension and gratification from their symptoms. The author of these letters—because his homosexual impulses conflict openly with his spiritual convictions—finds himself strongly motivated to change. Clinical experience has demonstrated that this motivation plus conscious feelings of guilt increase significantly the probability of therapeutic success.

Though the book contains some misconceptions about how psychiatry works (misconceptions common among laymen) the overall approach to psychiatry I believe to be constructive.

The struggle of the author to resolve deep-seated conflicts within himself and his progress (with a number of relapses) from a state of whining self-pity to a certain level of emotional and spiritual maturity will provide for many readers a source of understanding and for others a source of encouragement.

ARMAND M. NICHOLI II, M.D.
PSYCHIATRIST
HARVARD MEDICAL SCHOOL

Introduction

'If I had any guts I should write and publish my sexual autobiography, for the benefit of other poor devils.' Thus T. H. White, in a letter to a friend in 1936. The uninhibited sixties have given greater freedom to homosexuals like White who want to put their experiences in print; but by no means all of them do so with the aims of that compassionate man, and few, if any, have written with a combination of the motive which was his and a philosophy which emphatically was not – that of a definite, biblical, and practical Christian faith.

Yet by the mere law of averages there must be thousands of Christian men who are facing the problem of homosexuality either in themselves or in others who look to them for help, and who feel embarrassed, puzzled, or frightened by it and quite inadequate to cope with it. Among the sufferers there will of course be those who know all too much about it from their own past experience, and among their counsellors there will be those who have had occasion to investigate the matter in some depth. There is certainly no lack of information for those who want it. I have before me a recent copy of one of the 'quality Sundays' in which two of the three plays reviewed, and three of the major books, deal blatantly with homosexuality. Academic studies of the subject are readily available on the psychology and sociology shelves of any public library. But this book does not set out to provide information so much as help – help by sympathy. I write as a Christian who has tried to apply his faith to his practice in this area of life as in others, and I dare to hope that some account of my attempt to face the problem may be of value to other Christians similarly placed.

These letters are accordingly a piece of 'sexual autobiography'. There are alterations in names and other such details, and the epistolary form itself is a literary device imposed on the facts, for Peter and I have never corresponded on this subject, though we have often conversed about it. But the substance of the book is autobiographical, and consequently it has certain features which should be noted at the outset.

First, it is *progressive*, in the sense that as the relationship between Peter and me, and my understanding of that relationship, have both developed over a period, so their development is reflected in the letters. For example, because my own homosexuality is of a rather emotional and introspective kind, there is at the beginning a note of complaining self-pity, like the querulousness of an unmarried woman who has not yet come to terms with spinsterhood; and in the course of the correspondence this is (I trust) gradually overcome, though not without occasional relapses. It should be borne in mind, therefore, that the earlier letters do not necessarily reflect mature attitudes, but are to be understood in conjunction with the later ones.

Secondly, it is by the same token *individual*. Just as no two sets of fingerprints are identical, so there are as many different types of homosexuality as there are homosexuals. It follows that because these letters are autobiographical they cannot possibly be a comprehensive survey of the many varieties of this condition. The reader may be a homosexual,

THE RETURNS OF LOVE

as I am, but he will certainly find that his experiences do not
tally with mine in every respect; he may even find that there
is very little resemblance indeed. In spite of this, I trust that
at some point or other my story will coincide with the story of
a sufficient number of fellow-homosexuals to make the telling of it worth while.

Thirdly, it aims to be *biblical,* and in this respect it should
prove to be more generally applicable than if it were merely
an account of personal experience. The part of the jungle
where I am lost may be miles away from the part where you
are lost, but the same map and compass can help us both.
That map and compass I take to be the Word of God, both
Christ the living Word and Scripture the written Word.
Why do people who are otherwise thoughtful and sincere
find it so easy to break the third commandment? They take
the name of the Lord, and call themselves 'Christians'; yet
they take it in vain, by emptying it of what is necessarily
contained within it. The only Christ I can accept is not the
tenth-hand Christ of the popular imagination, but the first-
hand Christ of the New Testament, and once I admit Him I
find I have to admit a whole range of teaching which is in-
separable from Him – not only His own as reported in the
Gospels, but that of the prophets whom He upheld and rati-
fied, and that of the apostles whom He taught and com-
missioned: in other words, biblical revelation as a whole. It
is on the principles the Bible lays down that I try to base my
belief and behaviour in general, and therefore my attitude to
the matter discussed in this book in particular.

Lastly, because what I have written here is autobiographical, it is also in the nature of the case *unfinished.*
Although conclusions are reached on this or that topic of
enquiry, there is no conclusion to the story as such. No
magical formula is found to spirit the problem out of exist-

11

ence, no Alexander arrives to cut the Gordian knot. Still the struggle goes on, so that at times when emotion is uppermost I complain bitterly about the cruel Providence which is subjecting me to this incessant tension between law and lust. But when reason takes charge, I realize how much my experience has taught me, and is still teaching me, about trust in a God who is all love, and who yet for His own very good reasons has seen fit to allow deformity, pain, and hardship to continue in this world until the day of the restoration of all things.

The American poet Walt Whitman poured out his emotional heart in a series of love affairs with young men, one of which is almost certainly referred to in the quotation at the beginning of this book. 'I loved a certain person ardently and my love was not return'd . . .'. This is how it is with Peter and me. There is, of course, a true love between us, the love which is a hallmark of the Christian brotherhood (1 John 3:14), and in virtue of which Peter cares for me as deeply as I care for him; but the other kind of love, the grand romantic passion, is all one way. It reaches out from me to Peter, and is not returned. And yet in the goodness of God there *are* returns: 'the pay is certain one way or another'. I am not repaid with the sexual liaison which my flesh desires, but I am repaid with a gift far more precious, a new lesson about divine providence and mercy, and 'out of that I have written these songs'. For unrequited love is a form of suffering, and all suffering when invested wisely brings returns. 'God has promised to heal my body. . . . He hasn't told me if it'll be in this life or after the resurrection from the dead. He's promised me that I'll have a perfect body without any pain then. He could heal me today if He wanted to. But I can see why He hasn't done so far. There's people I can help and talk to that you couldn't.' The infirmity of that man, whose words are quoted in a little book of David Sheppard's,[1] is different from mine, but its rich rewards are the same – a God-given comfort in our own affliction (as the apostle Paul puts it) with which we may be able to comfort others in their affliction. Or, in the words of the Master Himself, when the corn of wheat falls into the ground and dies, it produces much fruit.

[1] *Arguing* (Scripture Union, 1966), p. 5.

One

Dear Peter,

There are no prizes for guessing what this letter is going to be about. Until I put it down on paper there won't be room in my poor brain for much else than the subject of our conversation yesterday; and as 'normal service must be resumed as soon as possible', and there are the daily round and the common task to be thought of, I must do my best to get things back into their right perspective. Maybe it will help if I write them down. I'm sorry you have to be at the receiving end!

But I would have written in any case, a letter of sincerest thanks for your patience and kindness in lending a sympathetic ear to the outpouring of my woes. Can you imagine what a relief it was first to be able to broach the subject, and then to find that instead of being shocked, or uncomprehending, or even (the most I might have hoped for) ready with some comforting stock answer, you encouraged me to carry on and talk more freely and fully about it than ever before? Thank you for being such a good listener.

I was ashamed at the time that you should have caught me off my guard – that I should have betrayed the fact that I felt so wretched. I don't *think* I talk a lot about myself, do I? At least, I hope not – so many people are their own favourite subject of conversation that one has to take seriously the awful possibility of becoming just such an ego-centric bore oneself. This biggest of my problems, therefore, this monster that lurks in the depths, is generally kept out of sight. *I* know when it stirs, but I trust that all the spectator sees is a reasonably unruffled surface. And on the whole this is what happens.

Nevertheless the Kraken is awake down there.

Of course you can be preoccupied for a good deal of the time with your work, and find that it really does take your mind off yourself. Even so you can hardly help but have some leisure; and what is to fill that? Well, a whole heap of interests, to keep your time and your hands and your thoughts busy, yes, and your emotions too. But what then? At the end of the most exciting game, or the most enjoyable excursion, or the most sublime concert – what then? You come home to yourself again: the embers are cold in the grate, and the house is empty.

Friends, then: friends are the answer. There must be folk whom you know and love, who know and love you? Yes, they are the next possibility on the list, certainly. But what Archbishop Lang once wrote has stuck in my mind ever since I first read it: something to the effect that in the loneli-ness of his bachelor life his great need was not for friends, of whom he had plenty, any more than it was for work, of which he had too much; it was for 'that old simple human thing – someone in daily nearness to love'. And that is pre-cisely it. Just as at some point you left both work and hob-bies behind, so you leave your friends, too, at the garden gate; and you're still going to be on your own in the house tonight. And brother, it's so *lonely*. . . .

In some ways this is the worst part of it. Naturally – and 'naturally' is the right word – the real answer is the one you suggested yesterday, when I had got as far as admitting the

loneliness, but before you knew that it was because I was a
homosexual. Naturally the answer is that I need a wife. Yes,
I do, I do! Someone to come home to, someone who will be
there when the rest have gone, someone to share the deepest
joys and the darkest pains, someone who will truly be my
'other half'. You were absolutely right: the answer is marriage.

Which is out of the question.

Peter, I don't know whether there's any way out of a predicament like this; and if there is, I don't know whether I'm
meant to find it. But I don't want you to be burdened with
my insoluble problems. Thanks again for being such a
patient counsellor. I said just now that friends don't meet
one's deep needs; but there is friendship and friendship, and
your kind I value tremendously. Come to think of it, yesterday in your unobtrusive way you were supplying the sort of
companionship I was saying I should look for in a wife! You
know, it's years since I've talked to anyone about all this,
and I don't quite know why I should have felt so free to do
so on this occasion; unless it was that we were both so
deeply involved in the trouble between Tom and Barbara
last year, and a subconscious memory of your concern for
them prompted me to open up my own troubles to you
where normally I should have dissembled and told half the
truth. So when my fit of depression and your sympathetic
interest happened to coincide, out came the pent-up feelings
of ten years and more – ten years of saying nothing but
suffering much.

And one does suffer. A crucified passion, like a crucified
man, is a long time dying, and it dies hard and painfully.
But crucified it must be. As Paul says, 'those who belong to
Christ Jesus have crucified the flesh with its passions and
desires', and I've had to learn to do just that. The 'flesh' re-

17

vives often enough, and from its cross cries out for something to satisfy it: 'I thirst'. Then *let* it thirst. I tell you this, Peter – however it may hurt, I do my best to resist that cry. Old-fashioned Christian morality may sometimes be an agonizing way, but it is my way. Oh, I grant that the motives for not giving in to the lust of the flesh are possibly timidity or respectability, but I'm not fussy! A Christian can hardly doubt that to yield to such things is not only displeasing to his God but in the long run unsatisfying to himself; so from both points of view it's worth holding out. And I would rather hold out because I'm too scared to give in than rely on some more high-sounding sentiment which in the event might fail me.

I feel I'm a child in these matters, and I'm glad I am, because I see a lot of sense in Christ's setting up a child as a criterion for Christian attitudes. Among other things, children need the security of a moral framework, and for them to have to grow up without a standard of right and wrong must be an experience as unnerving as that of the lost mariner, and as unnatural as that of the weightless astronaut. Give me the magnetic needle that says 'This is North', or the law of gravity that says 'This is Down', and then I know where I am. Show me the scripture that says 'This is Sin', and then I know where I am; and though the temptation to the sin in question may tear my heart in two, by the grace of God I *will* not transgress that law.

Peter, can you understand it? This is the impossibility of the situation – what I may have I don't want, and what I do want I may not have. I want a friend, but more than a friend; I want a wife. But I don't want a woman. . . .

This letter was meant to be drawing to a close three pages back. Forgive my having rambled on, and for troubling you with a problem to which I don't suppose you know the answer any more than I do. I hope you won't let it weigh on your mind; I should be sorry if it were to do so, for the mere telling of it has been an enormous relief to me. The fact that I have to live with it doesn't mean that you have to as well!

Yours with gratitude,
ALEX

Two

Dear Peter,

You're a glutton for punishment, aren't you? But as you make me the generous offer of an ear into which I can pour my miseries whenever they threaten to spill over, it would be an insult to our friendship not to take you at your word. I know you well enough to believe you mean it. I did say, it's true, that I could see no reason why *you* should have to live with *my* problem, and you have many claims on your time which are much more pressing, but I foresee occasions when I shall be only too grateful to take advantage of your kindness. Still, I'll try to keep them to a minimum.

I'm grateful already for your wise counsels; but quite apart from the way you spoke, I was much struck by the way you listened, and are ready (according to your letter) to go on listening indefinitely.

That kind of attitude, you see, seems so rare. If the church of God were what it ought to be, every Christian community would include those who could serve their fellow-members in this way. But even ordained ministers are not always prepared to listen to a problem like mine with an attitude like yours. It's a sad fact that there are pastors whose pastoral care stops short of the whole-hearted imitation of their great Example, who calls His sheep by name, so that they hear His voice and respond. *He* calls me by my name: 'Alex –

sinful, hypocritical, embarrassed, homosexual Alex', He calls; and in doing so He demonstrates both that He knows all about me and that He still loves me in spite of it. They, if they are half-hearted in their work as His under-shepherds, either know and cease to love, or love but fail to understand.

(I don't of course include the mere hirelings, 'whose own the sheep are not', and who therefore have no compunction about contradicting the Shepherd and saying that the answer is to abandon the old paths of righteousness in favour of some new morality. In practical terms, all that their 'pastoral care' amounts to is a cynical agreement with Oscar Wilde, that the only way to get rid of a temptation is to yield to it. But I don't want that kind of care. I delight in the law of God after the inward man, and I don't want them to accept and condone my sin, however much I want them to accept me as a sinner.)

But it's the honest, genuine pastors who occasionally turn out to be so disappointing. There is the man who is stocked with correct responses for any situation; they come out pat when you press the appropriate button, and it's with a sinking feeling that you pick up the little card which pops out of the slot, knowing that it's been pre-printed and that the rehearsal of your miserable symptoms was largely superfluous – in fact you'd hardly uttered the syllables 'homo' before the machine began whirring out its answer. Then there is the man who is quick off the mark not because he has no need to hear you out, but because he has no patience to do so. I heard of someone who invented a 'personal problem', and took his fictitious tale of woe to several ministers in turn, deliberately to see what kind of help they would offer; and he calculated afterwards that the average length of time which was allowed him to get going on his story before being interrupted was (if I remember rightly) *two minutes*!

Then again, there is the man who will quote the verse in 1 Corinthians 6 about 'abusers of themselves with men' not inheriting the kingdom of God as if it referred not only to homosexual practices but also to a homosexual constitution, and who apparently believes that 'homosexuality' and 'gross indecency' are the same thing. He might as well say that if you are heterosexual you must be a fornicator. What inexcusable, pernicious ignorance!

I realize all this must seem bitterly unfair. But, you see, I speak out of bitter experience. There are long periods when the disease does not in fact cause any 'dis-ease', and even when it does begin to make itself felt, it can usually be dealt with by some simple home remedy, such as a change of interest or occupation. But on the bad days, when you could weep with the pain, to whom do you as a Christian turn? Naturally, to your minister – who (you hope) will accept you as you are and listen to you as long as you want to cry on his shoulder, who won't interrupt you with a ready-made answer or a sickening slap on the back, who even if he offers no cure will at least offer care. Yes, you turn to your minister. And if you can know in advance that he will give you what you need, the limitless sympathy of a caring pastor, then you're a lucky man indeed.

Of course it is unfair to single out the clergy. In this respect they are no better and no worse than Christian people in general. Leaving aside those whom the church has ordained to serve as its ministers, you survey the ranks of the unordained, to see how many there are who have this pastoral gift without its being officially recognized. Isn't the number far smaller than it should be? How is it, Peter, that after all these years you should be the only one of my present circle of Christian acquaintances to whom I've been able to open my heart on all this? You will say that with us there are special circumstances – that it's because we have become close friends, because we have been able to talk over other personal matters, because we have been deeply involved together in this concern or that. And I grant that the grounds for my feeling able to open up to you on the present subject were that from experience I knew you to be the sort of person who would sympathize if I did. But that is just the point. The reason for my being able to share this most private of matters with you is that we have already shared other things, and found a kinship in so doing, a communion where barriers are pulled down and façades crumble; and conversely, the reason for my not being able to share it with Mr X or Pastor Y is that the existing relationships with them offer no incentive to go any deeper. Oh, I'm not asking for a society which has as its Rule No. 1 the public washing of dirty linen; all I want is a brotherhood open-hearted enough to encourage one to open one's own heart within it. Those are the 'special circumstances' in which our kind of relationship can develop, and they ought to be much less rare than they are.

So I fall under my own condemnation, and have to ask whether I myself ever bother to cultivate the leisurely, unshockable friendships in which other tormented souls can have the chance to unwind. You make me ashamed of myself as I remember burdened people whom I must at times have fobbed off with a cheerful 'Take it to the Lord, brother', because I didn't want the responsibility of carrying the burden myself.

Do come over on Thursday evening if you're free. Correspondence is all very well, but conversation is better.

Yours,
ALEX

Three

My dear Peter,

So it really has been sympathy, in its strictest sense. I might have known.

How loosely that word gets used – how often one says 'I sympathize' without actually meaning 'I *suffer with* you'. But when you said it, it was true. . . . Now I understand why you understand so well: you have been through it all yourself. One realizes that there are any number of variations in the homosexual pattern, and our experiences may well differ widely in their incidentals, but the basic problem is the same, particularly since we both look at it from the Christian point of view. So the scripture comes true which says that 'your brother Christians are going through the same kinds of suffering'. Even this kind; even you.

⌐ The more I think about last Thursday (and for almost a week I've thought about little else) the more clearly three things crystallize in my mind. The first is the depth and goodness of our fellowship together then. Although what we shared was no doubt painful enough, the sharing of it was pure pleasure. To have freedom to lay one's soul bare in that way is in my opinion – and in the New Testament's, I would say – one of the golden blessings of Christianity. But I only remember this as a general impression, for the details of our conversation have altogether gone from me on account of the second thing: your admission that my problem is yours as well, and indeed that you know it in depths beyond my experience. I don't quite know why this revelation should have come home to me with such stunning impact, but stunned I was, and even now I can hardly gather my wits to think beyond it.

What is clear to me, though, is the third thing, which follows from it. To be brutal with myself, if not with you, it is simply that we ought not to meet any more. For you see, I don't come to you merely as a patient to a doctor or an enquirer to a counsellor. You may well have guessed already (more easily than I would ever have guessed about you) that I'm strongly attracted to you, Peter; and I've long been aware that the day I'm drawn towards another avowed homosexual is the day I step out on to the thinnest ice yet. Well, that day has come. Up to now there have been very occasional revelations, as between patient and doctor, without of course any personal attraction; and much more often attractions without revelations, when I suffered in silence and no-one knew but myself. But this is different. We like each other, and now we also know each other, perhaps more than is good for us. Therefore it's dangerous for us to continue to meet. It isn't hard to imagine what these close, private conversations might lead to. When Paul says 'shun youthful passions' he's being no more old-fashioned than the human heart itself is old-fashioned. This is one of the Bible's most definite and practical commands, and also one of the easiest to despise. And without doubt it applies to our own predicament. You and I are both pretty well acquainted with the power of those 'youthful passions'.. Shouldn't we be wise to give them no further opportunity where we are concerned?

Dear Peter, it will break my heart. How can God hold

out one hand with the gift of a blessed friendship, and hold up the other to warn me not to take it? 'I give you Peter – you mustn't have him'? But so far as I can see, that's the way it must be.

You won't try to persuade me, will you, that an occasional meeting would do no harm? That would be disastrous. It's foolish to pretend that one can walk into such a situation and enjoy what is of value while neatly sidestepping what is dangerous. But if I know you, you'll be as firm and as sensible as I want you to be.

Goodbye, my dear brother,
ALEX

Four

My dear Peter,

Thank you for your prompt reply, and also for your readiness to carry on a correspondence, even if we do decide not to meet any more.

But thank you most of all for being candid about your feelings for me. You wondered whether you were being cruel, and whether it would hurt me unnecessarily to learn that you felt no attraction towards me? No, Peter, no – in the first place the pain of being told I'm not physically attractive to you is nothing compared with the devastating effect of your previous admission about yourself. (As I said before, I don't understand why I should have been so shattered by that. The fact remains that I was.) In the second place, the whole affair is put in a new light by what you have said now, that though we are both attracted to our own sex in general yet our feelings for each other in particular are on two very different levels. You say you wondered not only whether you were being cruel in telling me you could not love me as I loved you, but also whether on that earlier occasion you had been unwise in admitting your own homosexuality, in case it caused me greater temptation. But, you see, the former neutralizes the latter. Your experience of homosexual passion in other directions means sympathy for me : your lack of it in my direction means safety for me, and

I thank God for it. Indeed I would practically withdraw all I said in my last letter about the danger of our meeting, now that I can be sure that any advances I might make towards you would get a pretty chilly reception, and be doomed to failure from the start.

I know this might be construed as the rationalization of an underlying desire to cling on to your friendship at any cost. Having said we must part, the prospect is so dismaying that I have to unsay it, and I clutch at the straw of your non-response as being an excuse as good as any for keeping you. Is that what it all sounds like to you?

But honestly I don't think it's true. It may seem risky to maintain an outpost in enemy country with only one fragile line of defence, and prudence might advise withdrawal to a more heavily fortified position. But then God sometimes takes remarkable risks, and this one is by no means the first He has taken in my battle against sexual sin. For instance, more than once it has been simply not possible to 'shun youthful passions', in the sense that one enters quite unwittingly a situation of the kind one is warned to avoid like the plague, and then finds one cannot get out of it. There was an occasion when the current 'love of my life' (ridiculous contradiction in terms, isn't it? but you know how permanent these things seem at the time) was a man who worked alongside me in the same department. As my feeling for him grew more violent and harder to control, it seemed that I should infallibly yield to temptation unless one of us were moved from that section. Either he must leave or I must. But neither of us *could*; and there we stayed, in a state of unbelievable tension, seeing each other almost daily for eighteen months – and the Lord kept us from sin.

28

That to me is an example of how risky His procedure often is.

Mark you, I see not the smallest warrant for *our* taking risks of this kind. That way lies calamity. But if *He* chooses to lead us through fire and water, then He will bring us out into a wealthy place. To see something of His meticulous organizing of past and present, with all their complications, is to me a great source of hope. Isn't the doctrine of predestination meant to be a means of 'sweet, pleasant, and unspeakable comfort to godly persons'? If we believe in a God who works all things after the counsel of His own will, then having brought us to this place He means to bless us in it now and to make something glorious out of it in the days to come.

The element of risk makes me yet more sure of this. He must think the risk worth taking: He must have some end in view which is even finer than what He would have achieved in us by playing safe. And I begin to see dimly a little of what He may be doing in me through this relationship of ours. Here is a love springing up in my heart, as passionate as any normal heterosexual love. It yearns both to give and to receive; but as it cannot be requited, all its energy must be channelled into giving: which is a good thing. It yearns for both spiritual and physical communion with the one who is loved; but as it can never be physically fulfilled, it concentrates all the more on the mutual enrichment of spiritual intercourse: which is another good thing. It yearns for an exclusive one-and-one relationship; but what may be permissible between the sexes is wrong here, and consciously and deliberately it has to extend its warmth to others besides the loved one: which is yet another good thing. Of course these desires – to give oneself, to be a means of spiritual blessing, to care about other people

29

– should be part of the Christian make-up in any case. But they have been marvellously realized and intensified in my own case by the ripening of my love for you. Isn't that extraordinary? I know that some would say that homosexuality, not only the practice but also the condition, is morally reprehensible and should be abhorred and fought in all circumstances, and that I am wrong even to acquiesce in it, let alone to expect good to come out of it. In a way, I agree; one should groan over it as a sample of the perversions evil has wrought in the world, and long for something better. But if in spite of everything it is there, and the Lord apparently sees fit to leave it there, then surely my concern is to see what He can make out of such unpromising material? Paul's 'thorn in the flesh' came from Satan, and Paul longed to be free of it; but the Lord let it remain, and made it a means of blessing. It was a risk He thought well worth taking.

Even so, perhaps it's all for the best that I'm going to be away for the next three weeks! I shall write again before we decide about another rendezvous.

With love in Christ,
ALEX

Five

My dear Peter,

I've been taking advantage of this time away to do something I should really have done long ago. It's all very well to hold as a principle of the Christian life that experience has to be interpreted in the light of doctrine, and not the other way about, but when you're actually immersed in the experience yourself it's not so easy to remember that doctrine is primary. You are so busy either enjoying or deploring what is happening to you that you don't think about asking where it fits into the teaching of the Bible, and what God has to say about it. So I thought a holiday away from the usual surroundings would be a good opportunity to try standing back and being objective about myself and my problems for once. If in the next week or two you can spare the time to look critically over what follows, and perhaps to make a note of any comments that may occur to you, I shall be most grateful.

That mysterious thing called 'public opinion' is still puritanical enough (here at any rate, more than in some other countries) to make most of us homosexuals think twice before admitting openly that that is what we are. I imagine this collective reaction, like most public morality, has its roots in the teaching of the church over the many centuries when it really did have the last word on the subject of morals. In its turn, the church's teaching was derived from the Bible, even if in some respects it became overlaid or distorted by tradition. So there is presumably, even at two removes, some kernel of biblical truth at the heart of the general disapproval which has usually been accorded to homosexuality.

I suppose it's typical of a certain mentality to argue from examples instead of principles, and one shouldn't be surprised to find that the proof text *par excellence* which traditional Christian teaching has used is not a precept or a doctrine, but a story: the story which is immortalized (if that is the appropriate word) in the very name of the crime 'sodomy'. An apologist, however, ought not to rest his arguments on stories, because another apologist is likely to come along and claim that the stories mean something different, and then the arguments fall down. I see that Sherwin Bailey in his book on homosexuality [1] argues that the sin of the men of Sodom in Genesis 19 was probably nothing to do with sex after all, and that the Fathers of the church were therefore building on imaginary foundations when they condemned homosexuality because God condemned Sodom. Now I believe myself that their interpretation was in fact right, and that Bailey's is wrong, and the best scholarly evidence goes against him; but that is beside the point. There are sounder biblical bases for the condemnation of homosexuality than the story of Sodom, and these are what I have been more concerned with.

Sorry – that sentence is not sufficiently precise. I mean the condemnation of homosexual *practice*. What the Bible says about the homosexual condition is another thing, and I haven't really thought my way through that yet. But its

---

[1] D. Sherwin Bailey, *Homosexuality and the Western Christian Tradition* (Longmans, 1955), pp. 1 ff.

teaching is clear enough on the matter of practice, and one has no need to resort to ancient narratives to find it. Homosexual activity is prohibited by the Old Testament law, not simply (as some have suggested) because it was connected with the heathen cults whose influence Israel was meant to throw off, as in Deuteronomy 22:5 and 23:17, but because it was wrong in itself, as in Leviticus 18:22 and 20:13; and the New Testament lists it along with a dozen other unsavoury sins in 1 Corinthians 6:9 and 1 Timothy 1:10. It's true that the Bible is as harsh on many of the more 'respectable' sins as it is on this one, if not harsher, and the Pharisees who are vastly offended at someone else's lack of sexual self-control, and yet simply don't see their own lack of love, are roundly condemned as hypocrites. But that doesn't mean that the sexual sinner is allowed to get away with it. He too stands condemned if he is shocked by another person's hypocrisy or uncharitableness while he whitewashes his own sins. They still remain on the Index.

It can't be denied, then, that the Bible places homosexual conduct in the category of sin. This fact surely has a bearing on the common defence that such conduct between consenting adults is their own affair entirely, because it 'doesn't affect society'. If you could show that it really is a cause of social decadence, and not only a symptom of it, then to say that it doesn't affect society would be ridiculous, and you could legitimately class it as a crime. But that is neither here nor there. For even if it were not a crime, it would still be a sin. Even if it had no effect on society at all, the people concerned would still not be able to say with truth that it was their own affair entirely; because there is always a third party involved. The Old Testament says that these activities are an abomination to the *Lord*, and the New Testament agrees that those who do such things shall not inherit the kingdom of *God*. God is involved too; He is the ever-present third party. There is an area of activity which God labels sinful, and it includes many things besides those which society labels criminal.

It must be obvious to an unprejudiced reader that this is the biblical point of view, whether or not he agrees with it. Hardly ever do the writers of Scripture give the reasons which the twentieth century would give for the wrongness of an action. Marital infidelity is wrong not primarily because it has social repercussions – broken homes, deprived children – but because it means the breaking of a divinely-ordained vow. The enormity of David's sin with Bathsheba was not that it wrecked a marriage and caused a murder, but that it was against God – indeed, against God only (Psalm 51 : 4).

The trouble with these black-and-white statements is that man always wants to know *why*. He can't accept that such-and-such is not to be practised merely because it is 'abomination to the Lord'. So when God issues plain commands, without frills and explanations, He's accused of acting arbitrarily. Well, to demand reasons from Him sounds something like an echo of the devil's orginal demand, 'Did God say . . .?', but when you think about it He does in fact make some concessions to our curiosity, in that you can discern principles behind His 'You shall nots' in the realm of sex.

I think these become clear when you turn from those passages which teach that homosexual conduct is a wrong use of sex to those which teach what its right use is. It should go without saying that there *is* a right use. The idea that sex is nothing better than a necessary evil is thoroughly pagan, and how it ever gained a foothold in the church in the face of verses like 1 Timothy 4 : 4 ('everything created by God is good') is a mystery to me. Being one of God's good

gifts, it is not to be rejected, but received with thanks-
giving. But that isn't to say that the use of it is good no
matter what the circumstances. This, I take it, is Paul's
reasoning in 1 Corinthians 6:13, when he says that 'the body
is not meant for immorality, but for the Lord'. ' "Food is
meant for the stomach and the stomach for food" – and God
will destroy both one and the other'; physical appetite is a
biological thing only, and has no other object than its own
satisfaction. But 'the body is not meant for immorality,
but for the Lord'; sexual appetite can't be isolated in the
same way, because the satisfying of it is an activity of the
whole man (the meaning of 'body' in this passage), and he
is more than a merely biological being. So if sex is not a
complete picture in itself, but only one piece in a jigsaw,
the question is: What are the surrounding pieces into which
it will fit correctly? What are the circumstances in which it
is rightly used?

One way of arriving at the answer is by a simple and
rapid process of elimination. A man may have sexual relations with a woman who is married to him; with a woman
who is married to someone else; with a woman who is unmarried; or with another man. The Bible condemns the
last three – adultery, fornication, and homosexual practices
– in no uncertain terms, and is equally definite in approv-
ing the first; according to Scripture the sex instinct is meant
to be fulfilled in marriage, and conversely marriage has as
one of its chief objects (according to the Anglican service
of Holy Matrimony, following 1 Corinthians 7:2, 9) the
proper channelling of the sex instinct.

If therefore this is the only proper context for sexual activity, there is presumably something in the essence of marriage which the other kinds of liaison don't have, and for
lack of which they stand condemned. That something is

not far to seek, since the meaning of marriage is made clear right at the beginning of the Bible. In the Genesis 1 account of creation there appears the divine command to be fruitful and multiply and replenish the earth, and in Genesis 2 is the divine provision of woman as a helper fit for man. Here we have the two elements of procreation and companionship. So basic are these twin purposes that, in Old Testament times at any rate, a marriage which doesn't achieve both is almost regarded as a failure. (Notice that sex has a primary role in both, in companionship as much as in procreation, as is clear from Genesis 2; for when a suitable 'helper' is sought as a remedy for Adam's isolation, God does not find one among the animals, and does not create one in the shape of another man, but instead produces as the right kind of companion for Adam a being who is sexually complementary to him – not a pet, nor a friend, but a wife.) Then we add to these two elements the fact that marriage as God intends it is a permanent union: 'the two shall become one flesh'; 'what . . . God has joined together, let no man put asunder'.

In marriage, then, a man and a woman consent mutually to form an indissoluble bond (permanence) in which their sexuality is legitimately fulfilled by their love for each other (companionship) and their raising of a family (procreation). And this gives us a line on *why* the other uses of sex are in fact abuses. Take adultery: I might form what would seem to be a very satisfactory relationship with another man's wife. But measured against the standard of marriage, it would be a failure, because even if both the essential objects of marriage were achieved (mutual love, and the birth of children), it would be at the expense of the existing union between her and her husband – I should be building *my* 'permanent' relationship with her out of the ruins of *his* 'permanent' relationship with her. Procreation – maybe; companionship – maybe; but permanence becomes a meaningless word. Take fornication: I might be fond of the girl in question, but hardly with a view to a lasting bond (otherwise I should be married to her), and certainly not with any idea of producing a family – in fact, that's just what we wouldn't want, if we could organize things properly. Companionship – possibly; procreation – we hope not; permanence – unlikely. And take homosexual practices: not only is procreation impossible, but permanence is improbable (whatever my hopes might be; homosexual couples don't generally grow old gracefully together), and even companionship is not really of the right sort, since the helper that God says is fit for man, in this context, is woman.

So it appears that God's prohibitions in the sphere of sexual activity are not arbitrary whims. He has set up a standard, the ideal of marriage; and judged against that standard these other practices are seen to fall short in certain definite respects. And if I wasn't satisfied with a plain commandment against indulging my unruly passions, then I ought to be satisfied now that I see some reason for the commandment.

I said I was working through Christian teaching on homosexual conduct first, and aimed to come to what lies behind it (the motives and the condition) afterwards; but I'd better not go on any longer now. I hope you won't find the above too indigestible. As I say, your comments would be most welcome.

Yours as always,
ALEX

Six

My dear Peter,

I hope you won't mind the arrival of another long screed
when you've hardly had time to read, let alone comment
on, the last one, which I had to bring to a close with my
thoughts in mid-career. I was writing in it about the Bible's
verdict on unnatural sexual activity, and noted that the
stress is on *activity*: that once you make the essential distinction (for it seems to me imperative that the distinction
be made) between homosexual practice and the homosexual
condition, you realize at once that every direct biblical
reference is to the former, not the latter.

At first glance this is not very helpful. 'Scripture condemns homosexuality' is a superficial, ambiguous statement,
and needs to be defined more closely. But when you begin
to do that, and say 'We must distinguish between practice
and condition, and ask what is the Bible's judgment on
each', you find that instead of clarifying the issue, you have
complicated it – for the simple reason that while the practice is condemned, the condition is neither condemned nor
uncondemned: it is not even mentioned. So instead of having a neat, straightforward answer to your question, half of
it is not answered at all.

As I say, it isn't very helpful to have one's request for
explicit comment met with a blank silence. But it does make

one probe yet further, in search of some underlying principles. What I think those principles are will become clear in due course. But first the matter of the blank silence.

There are two opposite attitudes, common both in the church and in society at large, which seem to me to result from a failure to understand Scripture's 'No comment' on the homosexual constitution. Some have never realized that it does make 'no comment', because they have never drawn the all-important distinction between the two senses of 'homosexuality', and in their mind's eye these two senses blur into a single image which they can't get in focus and don't understand – all that they know is that it disgusts them. You could call this the attitude of *revulsion*. In contrast to these who make nothing of the Bible's silence there are others who make far too much of it. Scripture, they say, although it may disapprove strongly of (for example) male cult prostitution, has nothing against the homosexual condition; nothing, therefore, against the poor chap who (they say) is born that way; nothing, therefore, against his expressing his affections according to his nature, since (they say) he can't help it; and whatever Scripture may seem to condemn, it can't be condemning that. You could call this the attitude of *permissiveness* – like that of the kind-hearted Arab who one chilly night let his camel put its nose into his tent, and by morning found the whole animal inside.

Both these attitudes call for a good deal of consideration. First, the people to whom the whole affair is revolting, because they will not differentiate between the condition and the practice of homosexuality, really must face facts. Kinsey's statistics may have all manner of doubts cast upon them, but when Kinsey claims that four per cent of all adult males in the United States are exclusively homosexual

39

throughout life (not to speak of the tens of millions classified under the rest of his six-point scale, who are homosexual but not exclusively so) his percentage must bear some relation to the facts: those three million men can't all be fictitious. And presumably there are corresponding figures for Great Britain. So even if you don't count the culpable perverts, there are still plenty who can't help being what they are. And even if within that group you don't count the active homosexuals, there are still some of us who are neither perverted nor practising. Here we *are* – there really are men like us, with a certain peculiarity in our make-up which is in itself no more morally blameworthy than left-handedness. We are *not* necessarily pansies, or bohemians, or maniacs, or lechers. Many of us do our best to lead decent respectable lives and to appear as normal human beings, and some of us succeed. And so long as our abnormal affections are never expressed in ways which are against the law, whether God's law or man's, the law speaks nothing against us. So why should an ignorant society? Why should a Pharisaic church?

In saying that Scripture lacks any reference to the homosexual condition, I am not of course forgetting that some writers on homosexuality disagree. They have suggested, for instance, that this was one reason for Paul's being unmarried (1 Corinthians 7:8), one element in his affection for Timothy (2 Timothy 1:1–4); and even that this is what is meant by the 'thorn in the flesh' which he longed to be rid of but had to accept (2 Corinthians 12:7–9). He certainly seems to have felt towards Timothy a very special love, which included that of an adoptive father ('my beloved child') and that of an evangelist towards an outstanding convert ('my true child in the faith'). But the suggestion is that, because of a personality defect for which he was not responsible, the lonely old bachelor found the young man physically attractive as well.

Another possible example, for those who are eager to find possible examples, is the extraordinary intensity of the relationship between David and Jonathan. Here the orthodox view is that their friendship was abnormal only in degree, not in kind, and that this exceptionally deep but still non-sexual affection was expressed in ways which, though we might think them over-demonstrative and queer, were nevertheless customary for the times. Orthodoxy might also argue that neither David nor Jonathan was noted for his effeminacy – indeed, just the opposite – and that both were married and had children; though this argument carries less weight, since a man can appear thoroughly masculine, and indeed beget children, and still be to a greater or lesser extent homosexual.

But what do such examples really show us? Simply this. If these two close friendships had involved homosexual *activity*, we may be sure it would not have gone unremarked and uncondemned; but in fact the Bible says nothing at all against the intimacy of Paul with Timothy, and of David with Jonathan. We may assume that the relationships were perfectly normal. But even if they were not, still we could infer nothing more than that they sprang from a homosexuality which was constitutional but not practising. So whatever ignorance or thoughtlessness or prejudice may say, the Bible at any rate says nothing against the invert who admits his inclinations but keeps them strictly under control. Its attitude is certainly not one of revulsion.

But neither is it one of permissiveness. In fact the Bible takes issue with both of the excuses commonly put forward on behalf of the 'invert', the man who is homosexual by constitution.

The first excuse is that the genuine invert should not be condemned for homosexual activity because 'unnatural vice' is in fact for him a natural way of expressing himself. Against this the Bible sets the fact of *objective morality*. The invert may fairly claim that the hard words of Romans 1:26, 27 (a passage much quoted by those to whom homosexuality in any sense is revolting) do not apply to him at all, since they refer only to men who have deliberately 'given up natural relations with women', that is, to perverts. But having disposed of that hindrance, he is no nearer to being permitted the expression of his desires, because the path is still blocked by Leviticus 18:22 and 1 Corinthians 6:9, which state quite baldly that homosexual acts are *wrong*, with an intrinsic, unqualified wrongness. This is why Kinsey won't do as a guide to morality, for when he states that 'sex is a normal biological function, acceptable in whatever form it is manifested', he begs the question: he makes his moral judgment ('any form of sex is acceptable') on the basis of his statistics ('because it is normal'), although the statistics themselves merely tell us what people are doing on the basis of the morals they already have (or don't have!). By contrast, Christianity sets up a standard which is truly objective, because it is divinely revealed and therefore independent of human judgments or desires. 'As the heavens are higher than the earth, so are my ways higher than your ways and my thoughts than your thoughts' (Isaiah 55:9).

The second excuse is that the genuine invert shouldn't be condemned for homosexual activity because he simply can't help expressing himself thus. Against this the Bible sets the fact of *human responsibility*. The invert's 'I couldn't help it' is just one modern specimen of an attitude which goes right back to the garden of Eden ('the woman You gave to be with me, *she* gave me the fruit') and which is frighteningly common today. Of course there are areas where we are right to make allowances for 'diminished responsibility'; but we need to be constantly on the watch against the growth of these areas, for grow they will. It's such an easy way out to plead 'I don't know what came over me, your worship', 'I must have had a blackout', 'It's my nerves', 'It's my genes', 'It's my upbringing'; anything rather than 'It's my fault'. So easy, as a short-term policy. But in the end it will bring us to the nightmare situation which Barbara Wootton has called 'the final victory of medicine over morals', and which C. S. Lewis foresees in his essay on *The Humanitarian Theory of Punishment*, where the sinful are identified with the sick, crime is an 'illness', punishment becomes 'treatment', and it is the doctor who decides when – if ever – the 'patient' is 'cured': a society with unlimited possibilities of injustice and cruelty. 'Diminished responsibility' is a broad, attractive road to begin with, but it leads to destruction.

Again Christianity offers a contrast, the narrow way of *accepted* responsibility. We shall all appear before the judgment seat of Christ, to give account of every word, every deed; and I believe that the offenders who are genuinely, pathologically, incapable of answering for their actions will be far fewer than some would like to think, and that as a rule there will be no instance of yielding to sin about which we shall honestly be able to claim that we were not responsible. And that includes sexual sin. For how often can sexual indulgence be described truthfully as 'passion'? The word implies that I am 'passive': a power outside myself and greater than myself takes hold of me, and I am helpless in its grip. Certainly the Scripture warns us that whoever commits sin is the slave of sin, that the rigours of that enslavement are increasing all the time, and that there comes a point at which God finally abandons the sinner to it. But though he may plead at the judgment seat of Christ that he couldn't help doing what he did, because it was done in passion, yet somewhere along the line his passive submission to sin must have been a matter of active choice, and for that action he is held responsible. Not even the invert will be able to plead 'I couldn't help it'. Not even I shall be able to plead 'It wasn't my fault, Lord, I was made that way'. I'm a man, not a machine.

Well, that's how it all seems to me. At first, I must confess, I was rather taken aback to find no direct teaching on the homosexual constitution: I felt I needed it so much. But then it came to me that the relevant principles were these twin doctrines of objective morality and human responsibility, as I've tried to outline them in this letter. Two verses in 1 Corinthians sum them up usefully. 6:9 is a plain statement about morality: 'abusers of themselves with men' shall not inherit the kingdom of God. This is one of the activities which is wrong, however excellent your excuse. 10:13 is a plain statement about responsibility: God will not let you be tempted beyond your strength. You will never be able to claim that a particular temptation was too much for you, so that you were not responsible for yielding to it. Now if both those doctrines are true, it must be possible to hold out against even our kind of temptation, about which we tend to say 'This is exceptional – this is impossible – I can't help but give in.' No: there is *always* help enough to keep us from giving in.

I don't know about you, but underneath the appearance of being properly shocked, I find sometimes in myself a secret hankering after the freedom accorded elsewhere to practising homosexuals – in Holland, for example, where free from legal restrictions they have clubs which cater

specially for them. I understand there is even a pastor of
the United Church of Christ in America who welcomes and
integrates them into the life of his church, without a word
about their being expected to repent or forsake their wicked
ways. Wouldn't that be nice? But it's too easy an answer.
'In your struggle against sin you have not yet resisted to the
point of shedding blood.' It's no hard taskmaster, but the
sympathetic human Christ, in all points tempted like as we
are, who expects us to resist to the limit.

Yours as always,
ALEX

Seven

My dear Peter,

I wouldn't have plagued you with such prosy letters as the last two had I known what you were going through. I'm sorry you've been having such a rotten time, and sorry I aggravated it, unknowingly, by my pages of unhelpful theorizing. I must have seemed a regular Job's comforter. Don't you think that what surely disgusted Job about his friends was not so much that they gave no answer *to* his problem as that they gave no help *in* it? He wanted something practical – as you do.

But so do I, Peter. My symptoms may not be precisely like yours, though the disease is the same; but I can sympathize with your pain well enough. So, while the doctors may frown on patients recommending remedies to one another, I pass on for what they're worth one or two prescriptions which have helped me.

As a matter of fact, although what I wrote in those recent letters may not seem to be anchored very firmly in practicalities, I do find that the working out of the theory is in itself a help. Somehow it objectifies a subjective experience – takes the thing which is churning around inside me, brings it out into the light, compels me to look at it, and in doing so detaches me from it, at least for a while.

There's practical comfort also, I find, in the particular

matter I was theorizing about last, the doctrines of objective morality and human responsibility. They are singularly comfortless if you sum them up as 'God says: (1) there are certain things you mustn't do; (2) I hold you responsible if you do them.' But they can be put in a very different way. God is Law, and He sets His standards fearsomely high; but He is also Love, and in Christ He gives grace and help so abundant that it is no-one's fault but our own if we fail to measure up to those standards. Law and Love seem to move in opposite directions, but to such lengths do they both go that eventually they meet again on the other side of the globe. Because God's reach encompasses the whole world of morality, however far His law requires me to go His love will be there to enable me. In the words of the old hymn, 'the trysting place where heaven's love and heaven's justice meet' is the cross of Christ, but by the same token they also meet in the sinner who has been crucified with Christ; in him too the infinite demands of righteousness are fulfilled by the infinite resources of mercy. So when the pain is hurting almost uncontrollably, we can at least cling to the knowledge that it is never in fact out of His control.

This tremendous, all-governing power is the source of another medicine which I find useful. If nothing in the moral sphere is beyond His control, the same is true in the historical process. What else is the Bible story but the record of His sovereign acts in human history? At the beginning of Genesis the universe comes into being, and until evil enters to contaminate it, it is altogether 'very good'. At the end of Revelation the whole created order, good though it originally was, is replaced by something yet finer. You look at a beautiful thing in this world: God says that it is merely a foretaste of the beauties of the world to come. Doesn't that make heaven desirable? Then you look at something in this creation which Satan has twisted and warped: God says that that also will in the end be re-created in flawless splendour. Doesn't that make heaven even more desirable? Shouldn't a sight of the damage evil has wrought fill us not only with anger and disgust, but also with a longing for the day of the restoration of all things? For me, at any rate, it is an antidote against my own tormenting experience of the perversions of this world to dwell on the perfections of the next.

Sometimes it's despair which drives me to this remedy. You must know, as I do, how the repeated failures or the unremitting struggles wring from you the complaint 'How long, Lord? Is there *never* to be an end?' And the New Testament replies with the great doctrine of the resurrection of the body. Romans 8:10, 11 is one of the relevant passages. It argues, first, that the eternal life bestowed by Christ when He enters a man's heart is for the time being life for his spirit only, and not life for his body, which because of its sinfulness remains 'dead', that is mortal. But secondly it promises that, as God raised Jesus *bodily* from the dead, so He will eventually give life to our *bodies* as well. This very body of ours, whose faults and infirmities cause us so much trouble in this world, will be raised and re-created in perfection for the world to come. 'He shall change the body of our humiliation to be like His glorious body, by the power which enables Him even to subdue all things to Himself' (Philippians 3:21). It's the subduing I long for, the subduing and re-ordering of these uncontrollable bodily desires which are God's original creation gone wrong. And it will come. The fact that the Spirit already dwells in me, so that in spite of frequent failure I truly do delight in the law of God after the inward man, is the guarantee that one day the renewal of the body will follow. And the sooner the better, say I; roll on eternity!

Just think – there must be tens of thousands of God's people who in past ages have been through the same burning torment that we go through, constantly fighting against our kind of temptation and trying like the saints in Hebrews 11 to 'quench raging fire', and longing for deliverance from the weakness of this mortal body. *And they have been delivered.* They stand now before the throne of God in heaven; and in the Lord's good time we shall be there too, and the pains of this life will be like a dream that vanishes with the waking day. Doesn't that help a little bit, Peter? Doesn't that encourage you to hold on just a little longer, when in the depth of depair you feel like giving up for good?

> And when the strife is fierce, the warfare long,
> Steals on the ear the distant triumph-song,
> And hearts are brave again, and arms are strong.

Despair, however, is not the only mood in which I find it a help to let thoughts of heaven preoccupy my mind. Another is rebellion, when I want to shout at God: 'Why have You made we thus? I never asked to be born or raised with such inclinations; why should things be made ten times more difficult for me than for the normal man? Why should I have to suffer these abominable tensions?'

It's when I bring against God another complaint of the same kind that I get a clue to the answer. For I can with equal justification ask: 'If You knew things were likely to work out this way, why did You ever let me survive so long? Why didn't You take away my life before I came to learn the dreadful fascination and power of homosexual desire and my helplessness in face of it?' Now when I begin to declaim against God in those terms, you notice that I am regarding Him once more as an *all-controlling* God. The very grounds for my asking why He didn't end my existence before I got to my present state are that I believe *He could have done so if He had wanted to*. In other words, He is the God in whose hand my breath is, who orders the span of my life: not a sparrow falls to the ground without Him, and the death of the infant and the death of the aged are equally under His sovereign control – at the moment of His choosing He takes away their breath, they die, and return to their dust (Psalm 104:29). Since therefore I already believe (from other parts of Scripture) that He brought me into the world to make of me a creature who would glorify Him, I must also now believe that the carrying out of His purpose necessarily involves a certain length of life, which not only began when He chose, but will end when He chooses, and not before. And His plan for me would not be complete without the past ten years, plus *x* years still to come, during which I suffer the agonies of an abnormal sexuality. He has deliberately allowed it all to happen as part of the process of making me what He intends me to be.

> Watch His methods, watch His ways,
> How He ruthlessly perfects
> Whom He royally elects,
> How He hammers him and hurts him
> And with mighty blows converts him
> Into trial shapes of clay which only God understands,
> While his tortured heart is crying and he lifts beseeching
> hands....

Or, in the words of Scripture, 'whom the Lord *loves* he chastens'.

Hence the good medicine of a mind set on the life to

come. When I remember that one day my sanctification here will end and I shall be glorified in heaven, and that under the hand of God the finished product will be a splendour for angels to marvel at, it helps me to endure my present trials, indeed to rejoice in them. It can hardly therefore be called escapism. A better name would be faith: faith like that of Abraham, who knew that the land where he lived was a land of promise, not of fulfilment – his proper dwelling-place for the time being, but (as Hebrews 11 points out) a camp and not a city. He had been born and brought up in one city, and was looking forward to finding his eventual home in another, and he must sometimes have felt that life in tents was exceedingly uncomfortable. But faith in the promise made the discomfort bearable. So in the light of the next world I see that the torments which make me rebel, because God won't explain them, are mere details in the grand purpose which He *has* explained, the bringing of yet another son to glory along the same path by which the eldest Son went, the path of maturity through suffering.

Isn't it one of the most wretched things about this condition that when you look ahead the same impossible road seems to continue indefinitely? You're driven to rebellion when you think of there being no point in it, and to despair when you think of there being no limit to it. That's why I find it a comfort, when I feel desperate, or rebellious, or both, to remind myself of God's promise that one day it will be finished – finished in both senses: He will put a stop to the troubles of this life, and He will at the same time complete what He has been doing by means of them. They are neither endless nor pointless.

About the possibility, or advisability, of a meeting: I agree with you. I hope that by this time we are (like Brutus) arm'd so strong in honesty that the dangers will pass by us.

As long as we know exactly where we are, we ought to be secure. So I look forward to seeing you on the 20th as you suggest. The time will suit me very well. You'll have realized that in my last letters my thoughts have been mostly along the lines of providing antidotes against an illness, but I know full well that it's also a matter of setting up defences against a temptation, and I hope you'll be able to give me some practical help in that direction.

In the meantime, God bless and keep you. I pray for you often.

ALEX

Eight

My dear Peter,

I often thank God that ours is a firm friendship in more senses than the usual one. I like to think of it as having the firmness of a vertebrate body; it could so easily be boneless sentimentality, which would sicken you and be thoroughly bad for me, but the possibility of that kind of jellyfish sprawl is prevented by its sturdy skeleton of discipline and good sense and practicality. Our conversation the other evening was a case in point. In our predicament, after all, the crucial question is 'What's to be done?' and it's of real value to share as we have done, then and at other times, our practical experience of how the problem can be coped with.

Since we ranged far and wide in those few hours, it seemed worth while afterwards to try to sort our thoughts into some kind of order, for my own benefit really; but you might like to look through this letter and perhaps make comments or additions.

I think we both find that the indulging of the imagination, the welcoming and harbouring of wrong thoughts (which is the first step of sin, whether or not it leads to worse things), is specially likely in times either of idleness or of self-pity. The latter is perhaps the harder to combat, because even when you are guarding against idleness by keeping yourself busy, the regrets and longing for something you don't or can't have may still flood suddenly in and swamp your emotions. Then with the longing comes the imagining, and then the accepting and relishing of what you imagine, and then the sly search for fuel to feed these thoughts, and then maybe some attempt at realizing them in action: and there you are.

You find this dangerous mood of self-pity frequently arises in depression, don't you? I remember your saying that it's when you feel thoroughly down, for one reason or another, that you begin to feel sorry for yourself along the lines of frustrated sex, and immediately the first of the chain of temptations is there. In fact the depression might have nothing to do with sex originally: it could be the result of ill-health, or tiredness, or worry. I find this too, to some extent. I'm sure I give way too much to worry, and it often has this series of effects; whereas if only I could develop greater trust in the providence of God, by taking firmer hold of the Bible's promises, there would be peace in the heart to garrison it against depression, and the absence of depression would mean that much less opportunity for sexual temptation. You, I know, occasionally let yourself get over-tired, with similar consequences; the straightforward remedy is to go to bed earlier! All rather trite and superficial, but certainly the right answer sometimes.

With me, these introspective moods of self-pity are the result not so much of depression as of loneliness. Those two don't necessarily go together, for it may be on a day when I haven't a care in the world that the consciousness of my solitude descends on me out of a clear sky, and tempts me to imagine, and even to seek, liaisons which are imprudent or exclusive or just plain immoral – whatever is on hand to meet the suddenly-realized need. A tremendous help then is a wide circle of healthy friendships, and I'm grateful for those which have been given to me – with men like yourself who offer true friendliness without any danger of physical intimacy; with women, which have the added advantage of keeping open any chance there may be of the development of a heterosexual attraction; and indeed with children. I believe many homosexuals do find children specially (not unhealthily) attractive, and for what it's worth this too could be a foretaste of family life, and thus an incentive to foster whatever heterosexual elements there may be in one's character, with a view to eventual marriage. Even a company of friends such as that is no guarantee against 'the arrow that flies by day', the sudden reminder like a bolt from the blue that one's yearning for a complete companion after the Genesis pattern remains unsatisfied. But it does mean the arrow is likely to strike less often. And after all, it would be wrong to despise a friend for not being all that a wife could be. God made friendship as well as marriage.

Self-pity is a fertile seed-bed, where homosexual temptation flourishes with deep roots which are not easy to pull up. Idleness is a comparatively simple matter: the weed does spread more widely, but its roots are nearer the surface. Idleness, I take it, includes not merely the unoccupied evening or the spare half-hour. It is also the three-minute walk down the High Street from shop A to shop C, during which time the body is occupied but the mind is not, and between those perfectly harmless establishments the Enemy sees to it that there is a shop B displaying books or clothes or travel-posters which will serve to misdirect the idling mind. If I were to analyse the directions in which my own mind moves at such times, I should label them the emotional, the aesthetic, and the animal. The emotional temptation is the same as that into which self-pity leads me; it is sparked off by (say) the picture of a thoroughly *nice* young man, which makes me think 'How I wish I had the love of someone like that' – and there the fantasies begin. The aesthetic temptation is more common, and has to do with one's appreciation of a beautiful body, its face or figure. The animal temptation is the commonest, centred not in the heart or the mind, but in the loins – a reaction of sheer lust; which is where the others normally end up in any case. This triple assault is what I mean by the weed spreading widely in the soil of idleness, for in self-pity it is only the emotions which are affected. But then an idle mind is a vacuum, and anything will do to fill a vacuum.

For the same reason, though, this problem is comparatively straightforward, and the method of dealing with it is the one you have often spoken of, that of rigorous discipline. A simple method: which is not to say an easy one. If your eye offends you, pluck it out. If you know that a certain shop window, a certain magazine page, a certain television programme may be a source of temptation, avoid it, *avoid it*, whatever its other merits. You must 'mortify the flesh', put it to death: starve it, smother it, anything.

It can be said in so few words, and grasped at a single reading. But it takes a lifetime to put it into practice. What does 'mortifying the flesh' mean in experience? I'm ashamed now of saying what I said on an occasion you may have forgotten, that for me the hardest trial was the loneliness, while the carnal temptations I could more or less cope with. That was before you told me something of the temptations you had had to face, and made me see how paltry mine were in comparison. The Lord had certainly tempered the wind to the shorn lamb, whereas you had borne the full blast of the storm. So I take the lesson from a man who knows what he's talking about, and try to practise feeding the spirit at the expense of the flesh, concentrating on the thoughts of Philippians 4:8 ('whatever is honourable, just, pure, lovely, gracious') to counteract the allurements of the world, and filling those idle moments so as not to allow the devil a foothold. Wasn't that the meaning of Christ's claim in John 14, that the prince of this world 'had nothing' in Him – nothing he could get a grip on?

Some people would say no doubt that a campaign as intensive as this amounts to a morbid preoccupation with the problem, which can hardly be a right thing. But to my mind there is a difference between preoccupation and vigilance. Without vigilance there is no safety.

Would you differ in any of this, or add to it? I'm sure we covered more in our conversation, but you will have to remind me of the rest.

ALEX

Nine

My dear Peter,

The point you take up from my last letter is, I agree, worth more consideration. Had you not insisted on the possible existence of some heterosexual element in me, I doubt whether I should have given it further thought, but what I wrote about the cultivation of friendships with women as a means of keeping open the door to a developing hetero-sexuality was due to your sowing of the seed in my mind. Once I would have scouted the idea of marriage, as a ridiculous impossibility: you have heard me do so. I would be a lot less dogmatic now. Your comment on my case – that I had never given myself the chance of establishing a relationship with the opposite sex – would by no means apply to every homosexual. But for me it was a valid comment, and has led me to wonder just how possible such a reorientation might be.

There is no doubt of the existence of a condition which for practical purposes can be termed bisexuality. Plenty of the notorious perverts of history have been married men and have sired children. Whatever the reliability or otherwise of Kinsey's figures, there must be some facts reflected in his conclusion that number 6 on his scale, the exclusively homo-sexual male, is a tiny minority, and that there is at least some heterosexuality in most homosexuals. This seems reasonable to me, because although there are large numbers of them who show no interest at all in the opposite sex, this can be variously explained by a preference for homosexual condition or practice, by fear of change, by non-availability of psychiatric help, or by unwillingness or inability to take advantage of it even where it is available. I understand there is quite a body of responsible opinion nowadays which is hopeful of 'cures' along this line, and aims at the ideal of a sexual urge redirected into marriage.

This is where I have to search my own soul, for one of the prime requirements in bringing about a reorientation of this kind is apparently the subject's own willingness; and do I really *want* to be different? God in His mercy kept me from being drawn into the grosser forms of homosexual activity, with their subtle power of sapping even the desire for a change. But it would be hard enough to leave the relationships I do know. On the animal level, they may be no more than fantasy, but on the aesthetic level the beauty of the female has at present no appeal for me compared with that of the male, and on the emotional level it is a man who has given me more than I could ever imagine a woman giving. And there's the rub: I could never *imagine* a relationship with a woman like the relationship I already *know* with you. To change would be to leave the known for the unknown, to set sail on an uncharted sea. So am I willing? Well . . . I think so. I take it that Paul's advice to converted slaves in 1 Corinthians 7 – to be content to remain in slavery if it seems inevitable, but if they do get a chance of freedom, to make the most of it – is based on a principle which applies here, and that while it is certainly wrong to acquiesce in homosexual practice, it may also be wrong, in this sense, to acquiesce in the homosexual condition.

Willingness is not going to be the only hurdle to overcome, though, because it seems that a 'cure' depends also to some extent on how old the person is and how long he has been aware of his condition. You know it's been a matter of ten years with me, and that no doubt would make it harder. (I wish I had known something about this when I first realized what was wrong with me. But I presume that in God's plan the delay has some purpose.) A third factor is the proportion of heterosexuality which is there to be worked on, as it were. I guess you're better off than I am in this respect, you lucky dog. But as you have said, I really know so little of myself yet, and there may be greater possibilities in me than I have hitherto believed.

The fourth factor is the need for psychiatric help in the whole process. I may well have been rather foolish here in trying to go it alone. Never did I think the day would come when I should be stretched on a psycho's couch! But if such help is available, I'm beginning to think I really ought to take advantage of it, as a Christian duty if nothing more. We must talk about it next time we meet.

As you say in your letter, to achieve the goal of a happy marriage would not automatically remove homosexual temptation. Knowing that there was a good woman at home would not prevent my noticing that there was a good-looking man across the street. Oscar Wilde let his eyes linger on his beautiful Bosie lying on the sofa 'like a narcissus – so white and gold', and poor Constance Wilde ceased to exist for him. However, one of the priceless blessings the Christian has been promised is the gift of discernment, and I pray that in similar circumstances I should be enabled to understand that all 'Bosie' would give me would be an impermanent thrill called 'being in love', and that 'Constance' would be – appropriately – the right and lasting solution to loneliness and the need for a sexual outlet. Unromantic, maybe, and I don't relish the prospect of being married to a wife with whom I am not as deeply in love (whatever that may mean) as I am with you. But at least marriage would be something . . . .

Yet see what a warped judgment I betray, in the very act of talking about discernment. Doesn't Screwtape, in C. S. Lewis's book, point out that when men compare marriage and romantic love, it is the rankest folly for them to value the first ('the intention of loyalty to a partnership for mutual help, for the preservation of chastity, and for the transmission of life') less than the second ('a storm of emotion')? Marriage would be immeasurably greater than a mere something: it would be a wonderful thing, and a profound thing, and perhaps the Lord would give the other thing too, in time, as a bonus. How seldom we expect bonuses from Him, in spite of His plain declaration that He is able to do far more abundantly than all that we ask or think.

Later

Fine words. No doubt all very true: but as a matter of practical politics . . . ? I was called away at the end of the last paragraph, and have just been re-reading to see where I'd got to. And the whole thing is too impersonal. There are practical difficulties besides these psychological, theoretical ones. *What about the girl?* Because isn't the very object of the exercise a relationship with an actual person? It's hard even to envisage such a relationship, and it will be harder still to embark on it, but think of the complicated operation which must come after that! On the one hand I must be careful not to go too far: must respect her as a person, must not use her as a mere prescription to remedy my ills, must not play with her affections, dare not encourage her to think in terms of marriage until she is certain that I might be the right partner for her. On the other hand I must go far enough for her to have the proper grounds for such a certainty — far enough, that is, for her to get to know me as intimately as you do, for it would be wrong to expect her to make decisions on any slighter knowledge. Yet the deeper our intimacy, the more she will suffer if it finally comes to nothing. So how on earth can I explore the possibilities and yet guard her against the dangers? I don't know. I suppose it can be done — one foot on the accelerator, the other on the brake! At any rate, I'm prepared to keep an open mind on the subject; and should the wisdom of God deny me this solution, the grace of God will be sufficient to bring about a better one.

Your brother as always, but (I hope)
someone else's husband,
ALEX

Ten

My dear Peter,

You express exactly my sentiments about psychiatrists. I have
to admit to an instinctive distrust of them. It may well be
little more than the irrational suspicion the layman feels towards the expert in any subject; on the other hand it may
spring from a rooted objection to labels which masquerade
as solutions – I mean the idea that once you have labelled a
man 'schizophrenic', for example, you have thereby answered his problem. The psychiatrist I fear (though there's
probably no such person : I do the tribe an injustice) is one
who will listen to my tale of woe and will then say com-
placently 'You are like this because in childhood you were
dropped on your head.' So what? I want to be cured, not
classified.

What a caricature! Don't take it too seriously. In point of
fact, I'm sure that the provision of psychiatric care is essential to the welfare of the community these days. I'm equally
sure that psychotherapy can be a help to people with our
problem. There can certainly be value in uncovering the
causes of one's condition, provided it is only a means to an
end, and leads on to something constructive. I wonder what
are the causes of yours and of mine? Probably not physical,
in spite of the common use of the term 'invert' to denote one
whose homosexuality is supposed to be inborn. If it ever
does start way back among the genes and chromosomes, the

'invert' who wishes to shrug off responsibility has a convenient excuse for doing so. But I understand (though I confess to almost total ignorance of this branch of biology) that present studies find little evidence that homosexuality is a matter of genetics, or hormonal imbalance, or that sort of thing. It's much more likely to be environmental or psychological than physical.

Which of those was the causation in my case I don't know. I can see that, as you say in your last letter, yours was probably a combination of the two, a tendency established by psychological factors in your family background and sparked into activity by environmental factors later on. Reading between the lines in the biography of T. H. White, who seems to me a desperately sad example of a homosexual trying to master his affections without the help of the grace of God, I should say that it was because these two tides met in him that the flood rose so high in his soul – a difficult situation in childhood and dangerous company in young manhood, both classics of their kind.[1] For myself, as the various possibilities pass under review most, if not all, seem as if they should be rejected. Am I fleeing from a hostile father? rebelling against 'smother-love'? clinging to parental apron-strings and never growing into adult heterosexuality? seeking emotional refuge from the insecurity of a broken home? At first glance none of them really fits, but a psychoanalyst might unearth some such item of which my conscious mind is not aware. Or he might take it further back and find in the first few months of life, or even in the birth-process itself, reasons for a reaction against the mother and thus against woman in general.

---

[1] Sylvia Townsend Warner, *T. H. White* (Jonathan Cape: Chatto and Windus, 1967), pp. 28, 41.

Another excuse which may be made for not putting one-self into the hands of a psychiatrist, is that affection for parents makes one hesitate to start looking for a skeleton in the cupboard. If there is no obvious reason for blaming them, it seems a pity to jeopardize the family harmony by bringing one to light. But to hesitate on those grounds would show that one either did not know or else did not trust the survival-power of love within a Christian family.

Yes, I think I should be prepared to go ahead.

After all, it might not be an unwitting psychological wound inflicted by my poor parents at all. It might have to do with my environment at some stage. There's plenty of evidence to show that life in the services, or in prison, or in some comparable single-sex community, is very effective in making queers out of people who were previously normal, as you know only too well, and that an 'acquired' homo-sexuality of this sort is also possible through chance contacts which for one reason or another are followed up. All I can think of in that line is the usual schoolboy curiosity and experimentation, and the inquisitive fingers of some pathetic old man in the next seat at the cinema. Can a far-reaching trauma really result from such incidents? Then again, there might be something in one's environment (though not I think in mine) which could contribute negatively rather than positively to the acquiring of homosexuality, for in-stance an atmosphere of repressive puritanism against which one might rebel, and seek the forbidden experience deliber-ately.

I'm afraid these are thoughts written down without much object. You know a lot about me, but you don't know the roots of my sexuality any more than I do myself. To grub them up could be a comfort or it could be a pain, but either way it might be a help. I must find a Christian psychiatrist somewhere, if at all possible. (One wishes there were more of them.) Thanks again for letting me know what you think. You always disclaim the role of a giver of good advice, but you're an unfailing starter-motor for getting my own mind ticking over.

Yours as always,
ALEX

Eleven

My dear Peter,

In spite of your rap over the knuckles, I'm quite un-repentant. I still want the person who counsels me to be a Christian. The difference it will make will be more than a psychological one.

I agree, you see, that the obvious thing to consider is the man's professional qualifications. Of course Dorothy Sayers was right in maintaining that the actors chosen to portray Bible characters in her play-cycle *The Man Born to be King* should be chosen for their acting ability, and not (as was hoped by one old lady who wrote to her) for their piety! In the same way, for one's doctor to be a fellow-Christian would be nice, but hardly necessary. To the extent to which he would be dealing with physical ailments and not psycho-somatic ones, his religious views would be unlikely to affect the quality of his medical treatment.

I don't agree however that a psychiatrist is in the same position. So long as he is merely using objective skills in treating my case I don't care whether he's a Sikh or a Seventh-Day Adventist. But at several points it will be diffi-cult for him not to let his own philosophy affect his work. The question 'Tell me what's wrong with me' should get a plain answer, but the answers to other questions could easily be coloured – by the man's religion, if I ask what made me develop this way; by his ethics, if I ask what I'm to do about it. Can't you imagine a conversation something like this? He says: 'I advise you to do such-and-such.' I say: 'But that would be against my conscience.' He says: 'You must realize that your conscience is still governed by a number of primitive taboos.' I say: 'On the contrary, my conscience is governed by the revealed law of God.' Where do we go from there? I might still have confidence in him professionally, but it would have saved time, money, and emotional wear and tear if I had become involved from the start with a man who shared my own Christian presuppositions. In this kind of situation above all, I should prefer to be able to trust myself to my counsellor without reservations, and not to have to view his comments with a critical eye in case they disagree with my own convictions.

Yours as always,
ALEX

Twelve

My dear Peter,

I wish you weren't so far away at the moment, for there's so much I want to talk to you about. On the other hand I would rather you received this latest of my unburdenings when it has had the chance to cool by being written down, so perhaps it's all for the best that you're not within reach.

It's kind of you to reply with such calm good sense to my last letter or two, and you will not be surprised to learn that I am doing my best to follow the lead you suggest. I'm seeking psychiatric treatment; and I have a girl in tow. The latter is what this screed is about. But it's with some bitterness that I admit to following your advice, because there also I am pulled in two directions. In one way I feel it right on my own account to take this line of action: in another I feel it wrong, simply because it is your advice, and to follow it looks like the wretched dependence of a spaniel-eyed lover. Peter says it; it must be right. So you see my soul is in conflict. And to solve the conflict I turn instinctively to you — and thereby aggravate it.

That, as well as the girl, is what I want to write about.

In theory, it's all very well deliberately to embark on a venture which for most other men would come naturally, and to try to establish a link of friendship with a girl which shall consciously include the possibility of marriage. But in practice the problems are enough to drive one to despair. They're so unanswerable. I know plenty of girls who are friendly and likable, but I have now to look for one who adds to these qualities that of eligibility for marriage. That phrase implies a lot, for eligibility is more than a matter of your being certain that So-and-so will make me a good wife; it's a matter of my being certain that I should be happy to live with her, unreservedly and *physically*, for the next fifty years. And the unanswerable question is, where do I find a girl who will attract *me* like *that*?

Besides all this, of course, there is something we have discussed before, namely consideration for the girl herself. There must be respect for her personality and concern for her happiness. This is something which in one's selfishness one is liable to overlook. It is easy to forget that eligibility is also a matter of *her* being certain that the relationship would be right — that I should make her a good husband.

The coming of Mary — that being the lady's name : I don't believe you know her — has raised these difficulties in an acutely practical form. The need to show respect and consideration I trust I am coping with, but the rest I find almost unmanageable. I ask myself various questions about our relationship, actual and potential. (In the nature of the case I never expected to fall head over ears in love with her, so don't be surprised at the clinical approach!) First, are we in harmony spiritually? Yes; she is a convinced Christian with a living faith, we can talk about the things of God together and pray together, and we complement each other in our understanding of the gospel, hers being feminine and intuitive and mine masculine and logical. Spiritually we are undoubtedly on the same wavelength. Second, are we in harmony intellectually? Yes; we have similar interests, and while I for instance read more than she does, and she is keener on music than I am, we discuss them on the same level, and converse easily about most matters. Third, are we in harmony socially and psychologically? I bracket these together because what I have in mind is that we do in fact feel at home in each other's company, relaxed, free from the tensions which can arise from a difference either in background or in character.

So far, so good. Mary is a girl of whom I can almost hear you saying 'She would make you a good wife', and if weddings were made in the same way as wedding cakes, the confectioner would surely approve the ingredients of this one – so far. But the fourth question is the crucial one. Are we in harmony physically and emotionally? Have we felt the inexplicable magnetism of which sexual desire is perhaps both the cause and the climax? She says she feels it, the two magnets drawn irresistibly together. But I don't. I fear the one is magnet and the other plain iron, for the physical attraction is all one way. In my blacker moments I wonder whether I really expected anything different. No woman has ever attracted me physically, so why should this one? Oh, I persevere with the relationship, hoping that one day the obvious may dawn even on my dim sight, inspecting my own emotions regularly – still the clinical investigator! – to see whether I am 'in love' with her, or at least whether my mind is capable of dwelling on her physical beauties with appreciation and desire.

And then I go home and cry myself to sleep. . . . Because, you see, there is more to it than a failure to appreciate Mary. The refinement of cruelty is that she is actually being compared, to her disadvantage, with someone else. (I'm glad to be putting this in a letter, rather than telling you face to face: I want you to read it dispassionately, as I am trying to write it objectively, like Wordsworth's 'emotion recollected in tranquillity'.) Mary's lover will delight to make a fond catalogue of her features, though the rest of the world may think him an infatuated lunatic. Very well, then: we begin with her nose. Not a particularly notable nose, but a reasonable feature which according to some canons of beauty might be called pretty, though it lacks the classical perfection of Peter's, the width of the bridge, the curve of the nostril. Then her mouth – well, it's a mouth: the usual pair of lips and two rows of teeth! Peter's, of course, is something more; a beautiful mouth, its teeth white and even, its smile kindling pleasure in me like sunlight in a mirror. Then Mary's eyes. Nice eyes: I forget what colour they are, but I don't think they can be the same as Peter's, or I should have noticed it – that blue of summer skies which I have known all these months, together with the long lashes, and the way the corners of the eyes crinkle up when he laughs. And her hair, her hands and feet, her limbs and body, I can recall them all – once I have with a conscientious effort put aside from the forefront of my mind the image of someone else which rises there repeatedly, vivid and unbidden.

That phrase of Wordsworth's was a description of the source from which poetry springs, and I suppose one who had the gift would be able to turn my catalogue into a poem, a love-lyric in praise of the beloved. Not of Mary, alas – poor Mary – but of that other with whom I feel myself to be in harmony not only spiritually, intellectually, socially, and psychologically, but physically and emotionally as well. O Peter, Peter. . . . If I loved Mary as I love you, I should have proposed to her, refused to take no for an answer from her, and been engaged to be married to her, long before this.

Already I hate myself for writing all that. I have taken too much advantage of the offer of a listening ear which you made to me so long ago. I have tried to be restrained and objective, but with little success, I'm afraid. I know your own experience of homosexual attraction has not had this colouring of sentimentality; so although you are a man of your word, and will therefore still be reading, I realize that what you are reading must be distasteful to you in the extreme, pages of nauseating slop. And, as I say, I hate myself for it. On the surface it may not seem so evil a thing as an outright physical involvement would be; but sin is sin, and this emotional involvement is sinful, just as that is. It seems hateful to me, however, not as a breaking of the seventh commandment, but as a breaking of the first. Adultery is wrong, and Christ says that to look on a woman lustfully is adultery, and presumably the same applies to homosexual lust. But what is wrong in adultery is the isolation of the pleasure of the sex act from the total pattern of family life to which it belongs; and that is not what is wrong with my love for you. The trouble is that I can look at Mary's face, and yours is the one I see; it floats before me at my work, even at my worship. Studdert Kennedy in one of his verses cried 'I cannot get to Jesus for the glory of her hair.' It was an analogous situation. Whatever is allowed to fill my mind like that has become my god. And the Lord says, 'You shall have no other gods before me.'

Peter, I wish I could transfer to Mary the feeling I have for you. Then it would cease to be idolatry, because it would be able to flow on broadening and deepening in its proper channel, instead of being dammed where it is now, eventually to grow stagnant and poisonous. But the whole thing is impossible. What can I do? What can I *do*? You know I'm trying to wean myself away from you, Peter, and I hope one day you'll be rid of me, for I hate to be so painfully dependent. But unlesss I have someone to cling to just now, I think I shall go mad.

ALEX

Thirteen

Dear Peter,

I want to say how sorry I am for yesterday's letter, which you must have found acutely embarrassing. I had thought I was past that stage, but it just shows the dangers of self-confidence. I'm afraid I was looking only at the 'impossibilities', as your namesake looked at the wind and the waves instead of at Christ, and felt myself beginning to sink. The way the Lord stretched out His hand to rescue me was by bringing to my mind a very apt saying I once picked up somewhere, that when He intends to make something wonderful He starts with a difficulty, and when He intends to make something very wonderful He starts with an impossibility. Such a basic principle of Christian experience that one wonders why one needs to be reminded of it so often! 'God chose what is weak in the world to shame the strong.' 'We have this treasure in earthen vessels, to show that the transcendent power belongs to God and not to us.' You know how ardently one part of me wants to consent to my twisted desires, while another part wants those desires to be changed and corrected; what I have to learn as the immediate lesson is both to accept them and to resist them, using this area of renunciation and infirmity as a platform for the demonstration of the divine grace. 'I will all the more gladly boast of my weaknesses, that the power of Christ may rest upon me.'

I can't imagine what wonderful thing He intends to make out of this particular weakness, nor what audience is going to applaud the display of His magicianship in such a private, intimate theatre – unless it is the 'principalities and powers in the heavenly places'. But that's His business.

Forgive me for the hysterics, brother? You're a patient man.

Yours most truly and penitently,
ALEX

Fourteen

My dear Peter,

The booklet and your accompanying note arrived at the beginning of this week. It was kind of you to send me a copy. I had heard of it, and was interested to read it, though you were right in expecting that I shouldn't agree with it. Why are these modern 'Christian' moralists so keen to sell their birthright for a mess of unbiblical pottage? What is this soupy, ill-defined 'love' which excuses everything? How true, indeed how obvious, to say that one has to take into account motives and intentions and background in determining the rightness or wrongness of an action. But how easy to over-simplify that truth to the point where you say, 'I am not to be blamed, *because I meant well.*' Some time ago we discussed whether the morality of homosexuality was affected by its being one's inescapable condition. The question here is similar: is it affected by one's intentions? We decided then that the excuse 'I couldn't help it' was a pretty flimsy one, and it seems to me that the excuse 'I meant well' is equally flimsy. One's motive does not justify an action any more than one's condition does. Consider the motive, indeed, but don't accept it uncritically. In fact the more carefully the inspector considers the passengers' tickets the more likely he is to discover a fraud among them.

To start with, however, let's imagine that there are no

frauds, and the motives are all unimpeachably pure. In such favourable circumstances, if anywhere, the 'good intentions' argument should hold its own. But surely even here it is fallacious? For example, I came across the following statement in the report *Towards a Quaker View of Sex*: 'Motives and circumstances degrade or ennoble any act, and we feel that to list sexual "sins" is to follow the letter rather than the spirit, to kill rather than to give life.' Now I can see that right actions can be spoilt by wrong motives; but how can wrong actions be redeemed by right motives? Would the Quakers say that there are *no* actions which are wrong in themselves? If so, they would step out of line with Scripture. On the subject of fornication, for instance, there is that extraordinary quotation of Paul's in 1 Corinthians, where he takes the original statement of Genesis about the mysterious 'one flesh' which results when man and woman are united in marriage, and says (as if it ought to have been a matter of common knowledge among his Christian readers) 'Don't you know that this same unity is created even when a man has intercourse with a prostitute?' Whatever may be the depths of his meaning, he could hardly make it more plain that the transcendental oneness is brought about by the mere physical act, without regard to intention or motive.

But suppose the Quakers were right. Suppose it were true that an act such as fornication could be 'ennobled' if one embarked on it in a spirit of love. What precisely is this all-excusing motive? What is meant by this 'love'? The Quaker report remarks that 'homosexual affection can be as selfless as heterosexual affection, and therefore we cannot see that it is in some way morally worse'. But what is implied in 'selflessness'?

I try to analyse these high-sounding ideas in terms of the three kinds of attraction I have mentioned to you before.

Animal attraction – how can that be selfless? The burning desires of A's body reach out towards B's body simply in order to gratify themselves. Even if B wanted A in the same way, and A could persuade himself that he was consenting purely to gratify B's desires (what self-deception!), it would still not be the action of love, because it would not be for B's good: it would be encouraging in him the very selfishness A would be condemning in himself.

Aesthetic desire is as bad. Lascivious men call it 'appreciation', but that is a misuse of the word. Appreciation is a moral, legitimate thing, a stirring of praise to the Creator; self does not come into it. What they mean is a stirring of passion for the creature, an indulging of their own lusts.

It would be difficult to argue that either of those types of attraction could be redeemed by motives of selflessness. In fact neither is my own greatest problem, and I'm not primarily tempted to seek excuses for sodomy, the lust of the flesh, or voyeurism, the lust of the eyes. What I find the strongest drive is emotional desire. The other wants are related, of course, but what I want most is *you*, not as a plaything or a picture, but as a person. Now this, whispers the Tempter earnestly, is much less carnal, much more lofty a sentiment. Yes, say I, but equally selfish, still wanting, still demanding. I might claim that I could draw the line between the 'loftier' desire merely to be with you and the 'more carnal' desire to touch or caress or kiss you. It wouldn't be true, of course. But even if it were, even if I could draw the line and stay on the non-carnal side of it, it would be pointless; because the operative word on both sides of the line is Desire, and the attitude throughout is 'I want'. As Proverbs says, 'the horse-leech has two daughters, called Give and Give'. The family are all alike bloodsuckers.

Over and above all this there stands the God in whom we

79

trust. Because He is infinite, He is also mysterious, and some of His laws may well seem mysteriously harsh and cramping. But He knows best, and I am sure on other grounds that He loves me. So quite apart from 'loving' relationships with other men, what kind of loving response is it to God Himself, if, when He stops me putting my fingers in the pretty fire, I sulk like a spoilt child and try to find reasons for disobeying?

Mind you, I believe with all my heart that provided the Quakers' dictum is hedged about with careful qualifications there is real truth in it. Underneath every development in the homosexual character which the Christian must renounce because it is morally reprehensible, underneath all the indulgence and passion and selfishness, there is a thing which is not in the strict sense sinful. Don't misunderstand me. I don't deny the *evil* of the thing, for evil it certainly is, but I do deny the *sinfulness* of it. The homosexual condition is to be classified with disease, weakness, death, as an evil; not with gluttony, blasphemy, murder, as a sin. Both sin and evil are the work of Satan, were brought into the world at the Fall, and will one day be destroyed by Christ, but they are not identical. Sin, which we must avoid and need never commit, is represented in our situation by homosexual lust and the activity to which it leads. Evil is different. We pray to be delivered from it, but may nevertheless find ourselves left in it, and then have to aim at using and transforming it. In our situation that means a homosexual nature. I'm sure that in this sense it is morally neutral, and that there can be an affection springing from it which is, as the Quakers say, as selfless as heterosexual affection can be, and which ruthlessly stifles the faintest leech-like cry of 'Give, give' in order to give itself, silently and perhaps thanklessly, for the welfare of its beloved; and in this needy and unloving age it can be sublimated in all kinds of loving service. But if it is truly selfless it will keep the rules. Love is the fulfilling of the law, not the breaking of it.

Yours as always,
ALEX

Fifteen

My dear Peter,

I have indeed become aware of the dangers you mention, and I'm grateful to you for spelling them out so unambiguously. There was a time not long since when I thought the voyage was over and the haven reached. I see now that I was still in perilous waters and some distance from landfall. I was in fact only at the third stage of four in this uncomfortable journey, and you're right to make it painfully clear to me that I may not even now be home and dry.

You will see what I mean if I go back and chart from the beginning the course of my relationship to you.

Attraction was the first stage. It was simple, a mere matter of unreflecting appreciation, much as one might say 'What a lovely day' or 'What a beautiful view'. You happened to pass by: I happened to notice you. As simple as that.

At that point it was also, I judge, morally neutral. I can't believe that a manward-bending eye is in itself any more immoral than, say, an outward-bending thumb-joint – such things are to be discussed in scientific, not moral, terms (except in so far as any freak or imperfection is in the last analysis a result of the wrongdoing in Eden). It's like the difference between possessing a radio which is only tuned to a certain wavelength, and deliberately switching it on and listening.

Furthermore, for a subjective experience it was curiously objective. No doubt beauty often exists only in the eye of the beholder, and you wonder 'what he sees in her', or *vice versa*; but this seemed so obvious, almost *measurable*, as if no unbiased observer could fail to pick out of my circle of friends the one who was incontestably the most attractive.

Mind you, that image of you was not present and complete in every detail right from the start, like Athene springing fully-armed from the head of Zeus. It developed, or rather came into focus, over a period of months. During that time the contact between us had been increasing, and instead of merely being tuned to male wavelengths in general and to yours in particular, I was now actually switched on and listening – in other words, I had moved away from the stage of non-moral Attraction into another stage where the rules of morality had begun to apply. So I had to question whether I was doing wrong – whether I ought not simply to switch off and refuse to let the relationship develop further. Well, rationalization or no, I felt it was all right for it to go on, because the second stage into which we had moved was not sexual infatuation, but a far safer and more solid thing, genuine Friendship.

An essential characteristic of Friendship is, I think, that it should be *about* something. Whereas two lovers are pre-occupied with each other, two friends are preoccupied with some third matter of mutual concern. When, therefore, we found ourselves jointly concerned in the trouble that was threatening to wreck Tom's marriage, and went on from there to discover other common interests of more agreeable kinds, I consider it as a new dimension which the Lord thought fit to add to our relationship. It meant that of the bonds between us, physical Attraction became definitely subordinate to Friendship. What was more, we were able to bring out and share our sexual problems, so that they themselves became a 'third matter of mutual concern': that is, Attraction was made a means of nourishing Friendship, when it could very easily have been the other way about. My love could not be denied, but at least it could be controlled.

The next stage was remarkable, and I believed at the time, as I've said, that I had reached the end of the journey and that this was love in the completest form possible to me. It was as if by a chemical process the stable element (Friendship) and the dangerously volatile one (Attraction) had combined not in a mere mixture but in a compound, where the characteristics of both were altered. Attraction had its evil properties neutralized by the sheer goodness of Friendship, and in its turn gave to Friendship a depth and passion which were expressed in practical terms as self-giving service. And Service, I suppose, would be the right name for this third stage: the giving not of my body – that was to be guarded against at all costs – but of my *self*. I had already taken the risk of giving myself to you in the sense of exposing to you my inmost thoughts and feelings, with the result that in some respects you now know far more about me than anyone else has ever known. When in these circumstances you felt able to open your own heart to me, so that I in turn came to know a little of your deepest needs, it was a joy to give myself in another sense, this time as a helper and servant. All that I had, all that I was, was at your disposal. I would gladly have shared – nay, carried – any burden that was placed on you. What would have been a grudging favour had I done it for someone else was a willing sacrifice where you were concerned: indeed not even a sacrifice, because the giving of time or money or effort seemed to be not

84

a deprivation at all, but an enriching. Love was service, and service was joy, and I was blissfully happy.

But what I have called Service bore within itself the seeds of its own destruction. It was not, as I had thought, love at its most mature, purged of every taint of selfishness. It would have sufficed for some, no doubt, and the friend with whom I had come thus far might have been one who would be contented to have a servant wait on him hand and foot, so that we should both believe we had reached the ultimate in legitimate, loving, homosexual relationships. But I thank God (this ruthless God of ours!) that the friend He had given me was not of that kind. He was one who reacted in disgust against this 'love' of mine which was beginning to smother and stifle him, and in doing so he brought me through into the fourth (and I believe final) stage of my emotional journey.

What I had to discover the hard way was that Attraction and Friendship and Service are not complete without Trust. Even at the stage of Service, paradoxically, my love for you was by no means selfless. When I did something for you, and you said 'Thank you', and I said 'It's a pleasure', – well, it was, since it not only helped you but also pleased me; and for the life of me I could not have disentangled the two skeins of motive, how much it was done for your sake and how much for my own. In practice it was not enough that you should be served. You had to be served *by me*. The result was that I had to know all your needs, had to probe and pry, had to be in on everything, so that I could have the emotional satisfaction of pressing my service upon you. And what sort of a love is that? The only reason I write this now is not to inform you of something which must already have been intolerably obvious to you for a long time, but to make sure by getting it down on paper that I realize it myself.

So I have come painfully through to the stage of Trust, and am learning the hardest lesson of all – that where your well-being is concerned I am not indispensable. I'm learning to keep my hands off, to stop interfering, to love you enough to let you go. If you want me, you know where to find me, and whenever you need my help it will be yours for the asking, but no longer will I force myself upon you.

A strange bond, this, whose permanence depends on the *loosening* of knots! I think it is really possible for none but those who believe in Christ, since among unbelievers Trust can only mean trust in each other. The best they can say is, 'I love you so much that I will cease to smother you with my attentions, trusting that you will manage quite successfully without them.' But the loved one might not be able to manage; and the lover, seeing him wallow helplessly, might conclude in despair that he is indispensable after all, and so the relationship would be driven into a vicious spiral. For the Christian, though, Trust means primarily trust in God, and *His* reliability is guaranteed. As a Christian, what I can say is, 'I love you so much that I will cease to smother you with my attentions, trusting that *He* will manage you quite successfully without them.' I must learn to be like the centurion in the Gospel story, who was so sure of the power and love of Christ that he asked for (and got) a blessing for the sick servant 'who was dear to him' even without invading the privacy of the sick-room. It was done at a distance, unobtrusively, without fuss: 'only say the word, and my boy shall be healed'. I'm trying by the grace of God to maintain my relationship to you on that level. If it ever slips back, and I forget myself, be brutal and tell me.

Yours as always,
ALEX

Sixteen

My dear Peter,

You may well ask how I'm getting on with my psychiatrist. I often ask myself the same thing, and get rather confused replies! I think I was hoping that he would provide some magical formula which would simply remove the problem. After all, there are grounds for such a hope, for mine might be one of the cases where the exposing or re-living of the crucial traumatic experience (whatever it may have been) really does seem to set the victim free from its bondage. Some kind of treatment may yet do that for me. The prospect at the moment, however, is not all that encouraging.

'Hope deferred makes the heart sick', and I can see how the desire for a quick fulfilment of one's hopes could soon lure one away on a wild-goose chase. That was not in fact the original cause of my own excursion into the realms of psychiatry, but it could easily have been, and I'm sure it also leads some Christians into the realms of dubious theology. They dream of an instant uprooting of the evil within them, not in this case by psychoanalysis but as part of Christ's promise to deliver them from sin. It's due of course to a misunderstanding of what that promise really means. Immediate deliverance is only from the guilt of sin; there is progressive deliverance from the power of sin; but total deliverance will not come till the next world, when this body of ours is finally redeemed, for then its bias towards sin will vanish too, and so will its mortality and infirmity and tendency to disease. In the meantime the homosexuality remains, and the temptation still lurks, and barring miracles (which do sometimes happen!), one has no biblical reason to expect a foretaste in this life of what belongs properly to the next, and certainly no right to claim such a foretaste. There are no quick answers.

Even now I could lapse easily and often into the old feeling of self-pity. But feeling must give way to faith, and I'm driven back and back again to James 5:15, 'the prayer of faith will save the sick man', and the massive truths by which that verse is underpinned. For faith is nothing but a reliance on facts, and I just have to remind myself constantly of the facts on which my own prayer of faith has been built up over these months: as follows. Nothing is outside God's control (Ephesians 1:11). Whatever He allows to happen to His people, He is acting rightly (Genesis 18:25) and lovingly (1 John 4:16), for their welfare (Jeremiah 29:11), and for His own glory (Philippians 1:20). In this faith, I can face the prospect of my love towards you evaporating one day, and my homosexuality enduring for the rest of my life – although that prospect appals me, and I wish that the homosexuality would go and (illogically) that the love would remain. In this faith, I pray: I pray for His work to be perfected in you and me, and whether He plans to heal our abnormal sexuality in this life or intends to wait till the complete healing of the life beyond, the prayer of faith shall most infallibly save the sick, and the Lord shall raise them up.

So instead of casting doubts on His wisdom (which is really what I'm doing when I complain), I am learning to use my weakness as an opportunity to prove His power, and to revel in conflict because it holds the hope of victory. In this conflict all the weapons we have discussed come into play: conscience and Scripture, discipline, common sense, fellowship, prayer, love, faith, and hope. And also one I think we have seldom if ever mentioned. I should call it *perspective*. One of the devil's tricks is to fill our minds with immense problems which in fact only seem so large because we are too close to them, and which would shrink to their proper size if we put them in a right perspective. A few square inches of handkerchief tied across one's eyes will effectively obliterate the view of a thousand square miles of countryside.

Do you remember how shattered I was when you first told me of your own sexual history? And do you remember how I couldn't understand why the incident had that unnerving effect on me? I think on reflection that it was because love had drawn me so close to you; I was practically identifying myself with you – 'the soul of Jonathan was knit to the soul of David' – and to have suddenly displayed before me the explicit sins of my best beloved, the one I thought of as my own other half, was a shock I could scarcely bear. What I had to tell myself with great firmness was that I was allowing your guilt to loom unwarrantably large. It was appearing to me much larger (indeed infinitely larger) than it appeared to God Himself, since He had already forgiven and forgotten it, and so far as He was concerned, it no longer existed. If your activities have been sinful in His sight, my fantasies have been equally offensive; and if I have now been acquitted, then so have you. I still have to tell myself this, for Satan still sometimes parades the illusion before my eyes. I have to do with your sins what Luther did with his own, in that dream of his when the Accuser came to bring them up against him afresh – he admitted them all, then scrawled across the list, 'The blood of Jesus Christ cleanses us from all sin.'

And as with that specific instance of disproportion, so with the entire question of homosexuality. It has to be put in its place. Why should I let myself be persuaded that it is the biggest thing in my life? Why should such a slice of my energy-budget be devoted not merely to defence, but to defence on this particular sector? We have talked before about idleness, and how Satan will hurl the forces of temptation into any unguarded gap. But he can also achieve subtler aims by bringing up his forces against positions which are already heavily guarded, for by concentrating more and more on manning those positions we tend to leave others progressively weakened.

You don't need field-glasses to see the enormous power he is deploying on this front. It must sometimes happen that when a man first discovers himself to be a homosexual, he thinks in all innocence that he is one of a tiny minority. But the briefest investigation of the homosexual world might well drive him to the opposite conclusion, and make him wonder whether it is not the normal men who are in a minority in a society riddled from top to bottom with sexual perversion. We both know only too well, I from my reading and you from your experience, how close this is to the truth. A piece of research like Jess Stearn's *The Sixth Man* could scare me out of my wits. Indeed one of the people Stearn interviewed told him that one in six was by no means the true proportion of homosexuals in society, and that it would be more accurate to call his book *The Sea Around You*. One allows for exaggeration, but it *is* like the sea. Again the story of the storm on Galilee comes to mind: once Peter stepped out of the boat there was nothing beneath his feet but fathom upon fathom of murky water. *Facilis descensus*

Averni – easy is the descent to hell. What is to prevent a man sinking from one depth to the next, till in the end the weeds wrap around his limbs and drown him? Only luck – or grace. Grace, of course, is the answer, and when the hand of Christ gripped that of the sinking man it must have had the effect not only of saving him but also of restoring his sense of proportion. The heaving water beneath him, the Master who held him – which was really the more powerful?

So Satan blows up these things till men are deceived into thinking that their sheer size indicates their importance. I believe it's common for homosexuals to be obsessed with their sexual predicament to the point where they can think of nothing else, and I see the tendency in myself. A balloon which needs to be pricked, my brother – a house of cards which will collapse before a gust of good sense and discernment, and humour, which our solemn enemy can't abide. All these help to get things in perspective. There are more important matters in life than indulging in a good moan because one is made differently from one's neighbour. The neighbour may be envied for his blessedly uncomplicated heterosexual life, but he assuredly has some other burden he might justifiably moan about. And even with regard to my own type of burden, why should I complain that I'm particularly hard done by, when there are countless unmarried women who have to cope with similar frustrations and tensions? O ye happily-married couples, O ye disappointed spinsters, O ye helpless homosexuals, O *all* ye works of the Lord, bless ye the Lord.

With love and prayers as always,
ALEX

Postscript

*Thou shalt remember all the way which the Lord
thy God led thee these forty years in the wilderness,
to humble thee, and to prove thee, to know what was
in thine heart, whether thou wouldest keep his
commandments, or no.*

DEUTERONOMY 8:2

Why, Lord? Why these years in the wilderness, enjoying
neither the pleasures of Egypt nor those of Canaan — why
these hungry years?

Listen, child, and I will tell you.

*They are to humble you: they reveal your helplessness. They
show that you are a sinner in bonds; that what the world
calls* freedom *to do what you like is really a terrible com-
pulsion to do what you like; that this 'what-you-like' — your
emotional and physical desire — holds you captive and hur-
ries you to destruction, unless I come and set you free.*

*They are to prove you: they reveal your value. When you
consider the immensity of the heavens, the work of My
fingers, naturally you cry, 'What is man, that God should
care about him?' But I reply, Since when has mere size
been the measure of value? Know that it is man that I have*

crowned with glory and honour: he is the chief of My works, an immortal soul, a responsible being, and the wilderness years show that I regard him as metal worth testing.

They are to know your heart: they reveal your mind and your will. They show whether you are in harmony with My thoughts or at variance with them; they show whether you are rebelling against My law or willing to obey it; and in them it becomes clear that your heart is Mine.

Listen, child — you who are by the Fall a sinner, yet still by creation a man, and now by redemption a saint: these are wonders I mean to declare before the eyes of the universe. Walk with Me through the wilderness.

Yes, Lord.